Exploring Earth's Resources

Using Coal, Oil, and Gas

Sharon Katz Cooper

Raintree

www.raintreepublishers.co.uk
Visit our website to find out more information about **Raintree** books.

To order:
 Phone 44 (0) 1865 888112
 Send a fax to 44 (0) 1865 314091
Visit the Raintree Bookshop at **www.raintreepublishers.co.uk** to browse our catalogue and order online.

First published in Great Britain by Raintree, Halley Court, Jordan Hill, Oxford OX2 8EJ, part of Harcourt Education.
Raintree is a registered trademark of Harcourt Education Ltd.

Editorial: Isabel Thomas, Sarah Chappelow and Vicki Yates
Design: Michelle Lisseter
Illustrations: Q2A Solutions
Picture Research: Erica Newbery
Production: Duncan Gilbert
Originated by Modern Age
Printed and bound in China by South China Printing Company

10 digit ISBN 1 406 20622 9
13 digit ISBN 978-1-4062-0622-7
11 10 09 08 07
10 9 8 7 6 5 4 3 2 1

British Library Cataloguing in Publication Data
Cooper, Sharon Katz
    Using coal, oil, and gas. – (Exploring Earth's resources)
    1. Petroleum products – Juvenile literature 2. Petroleum – Juvenile literature
    I. Title
    333.8'232

ISBN – 13: 9781406206227
ISBN – 10: 1406206229

A full catalogue record for this book is available from the British Library.

Acknowledgements
The publishers would like to thank the following for permission to reproduce photographs: Alamy pp. **14** (Marie-Louise Avery), **18** (PHOTOTAKE Inc.), **19** (Horizon International Images Limited); Corbis pp. **9** (SABA/Peter Blakely), **11** (Royalty Free), **12** (Paul A. Souders), **17**, **21** (Royalty Free), **21** (Mango Productions); Getty p. **22** (Photodisc); Harcourt Education p. **13** (Tudor Photography); Jupiter p. **5** (Banana Stock); Rex Features p. **15**; Science Photo Library & istock & Getty Images p. **4** (Photodisc); Still pictures pp. **8** (UNEP/S.Compoint), **10** (Peter Frischmuth), **16** (Jochen Tack/Das Fotoarchiv), **20** (Jeff Greenberg)

Cover photograph reproduced with permission of Alamy (Mark Sykes).

Contents

Some words are shown in bold, **like this**.
You can find them in the glossary on page 23.

What are coal, oil, and natural gas?

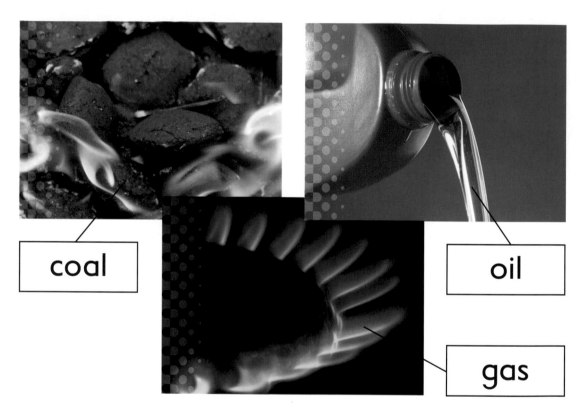

coal

oil

gas

Coal, oil, and natural gas are **natural resources**.

Natural resources come from the Earth.

Coal, oil, and natural gas are fuels.

We use fuels for **energy**.

What are coal, oil, and gas made of?

① rotting trees

mud

Coal, oil, and natural gas are **fossil fuels**.

They are the remains of plants and animals that lived long ago.

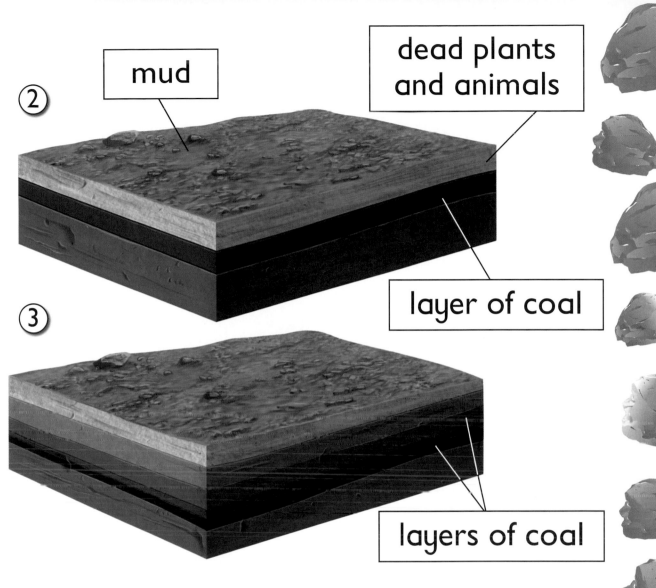

② mud

dead plants and animals

layer of coal

③

layers of coal

Thick mud covered these plants and animals after they died.

After a long time, they turned into coal, oil, or gas.

How do we find coal, oil, and gas?

oil

We find **fossil fuels** deep underground.

We drill deep into the Earth.
We pump out oil and natural gas.

Ships and big pipes move oil and natural gas.

They take the fossil fuels to places where we can use them.

Coal is also found deep underground.

When scientists find a place with a lot of coal, workers dig a **mine**.

Miners go deep into the ground and cut out the coal.

Special trains bring the coal up to the surface.

How do we use coal, oil, and gas?

Power plants burn coal, oil, and gas to make electricity.

We use this electricity to light houses, schools, and workplaces.

We also use **fossil fuels** to make plastics.

Many of the objects you use every day are made from plastic.

Some homes use natural gas for cooking and heating.

The gas burns with a blue flame.

14

Many people around the world
burn coal for heating and cooking.

We use gas, oil, and coal to help us get around.

Many trains and aeroplanes use diesel fuel. Diesel is a type of oil.

Most cars run on petrol.

Petrol is also made from oil.

Who studies coal, oil, and gas?

Scientists who study rocks are called **geologists**.

They look for new places to drill for oil and gas.

Engineers look for the safest ways to get fuels out of the ground.

Will we ever run out of coal, oil, and gas?

Fossil fuels are **non-renewable**.

Once we use them up, they will be gone forever.

To make fossil fuels last longer, we can use bikes instead of cars.

We can use different kinds of **energy**, like wind power.

Fuelling electricity

We use **fossil fuels** to make electricity. Look at this picture. Which objects use electricity? Which objects use gas? Can you think of four ways you could use less electricity at home?

Glossary

 **energy** something that gives power

 **engineer** scientist who knows how to make and fix machines

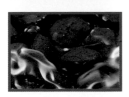 **fossil fuel** gas, oil, or coal. Fossil fuels are made from plants and animals that lived long ago

 **geologist** scientist who studies rocks

 **mine** place in the ground where coal is found

 **natural resources** a material from Earth that we can use

 **non-renewable** something that will not last forever, and will run out one day

Index

Titles in the *Exploring Earth's Resources* series include:

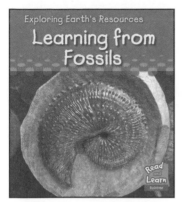

Hardback   1-406-20623-7

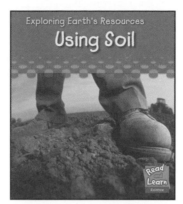

Hardback   1-406-20618-0

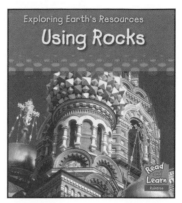

Hardback   1-406-20617-2

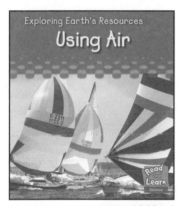

Hardback   1-406-20621-0

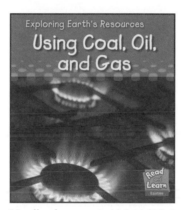

Hardback   1-406-20622-9

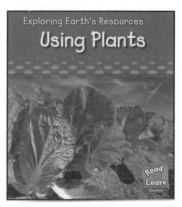

Hardback   1-406-20619-9

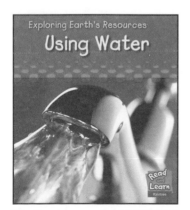

Hardback   1-406-20620-2

Find out about the other titles in this series on our website www.raintreepublishers.co.uk